LOW CARB CHOCOLATE RECIPES

Low carbohydrate, sugar free and gluten free

GEORGINA BOMER

Low Carb Chocolate Recipes by Georgina Bomer

www.stepawayfromthecarbs.com
www.georginabomer.com

Other books by this author:

Low Carb Family Favorites
Low Carb Snacks
Low Carb Meals For One

CONTENTS

INTRODUCTION

My first book, The Dieter's Chocolate Cookbook, was published back in 2011 and continues to sell well. Readers loved the recipes and the information given, but I was repeatedly asked for a photo of each recipe. I agreed with them, and I was determined that my next recipe book would have color images!

Also the format of the original book incorporated recipes for those following low carb, low fat, low calorie and sugar free diets. Not every recipe was suitable for every diet, so it was a mix and match plan. Although versatile, it was also confusing, so this second book has been streamlined to include only low carbohydrate and sugar free diets from the original four. I have, however, added icons to show that all recipes are gluten-free and many are lactose-free.

In 2014 I founded the blog stepawayfromthecarbs.com – where I share new low carb recipes, product reviews and general information several times a week. If you are committed to the low carb way of eating, I highly recommend that you check it out, and sign up for my newsletter. Or follow me on Facebook, Twitter, Pinterest or Instagram! I would love the opportunity to connect with you and get feedback on this book.

GB

www.facebook.com/stepawayfromthecarbs/
www.twitter.com/stepawaycarbs
www.pinterest.com/stepawaycarbs/
www.instagram.com/stepawayfromthecarbs/

Different diets

The recipes featured in this book are all low carbohydrate, sugar free and gluten free. Many recipes are also lactose free, and all are indicated by the icons below:

In addition, the nutritional data is listed for every recipe so that you can make your own decision about whether it is suitable. If you change any of the ingredients the nutritional data will need to be recalculated.

Net carbohydrates, fiber, and the differences between the USA and UK/Australia

Most low carbohydrate diets count the carbs that can be digested, as these are the ones that affect blood sugar levels.

In the US, fiber is considered part of the carbohydrate content in the nutritional data tables on commercial products. However, fiber is not digestible and therefore the amount of fiber should be subtracted from the total carbohydrates in order to get the "net carbs" amount.

In the UK and Australia, fiber (fibre) is treated separately, so the carbohydrate count listed on commercial products does not include the fiber, and is already net.

In this book, total carbohydrates, fiber, and net carbohydrates are listed separately for clarity.

Serving size

Every effort has been made to give reasonable portion sizes in this book. All too often, diet recipes produce inadequate portions in order to make the nutritional data look attractive. However, these are intended to be treats in addition to a balanced diet.

Yield

Recipes in this book serve a variety of yields. Some recipes will make just one serving (like a hot chocolate drink), others will make a larger yield (a batch of cookies or a cake). Most recipes with a smaller yield can be increased easily, with suitable adjustments for cooking time, if applicable.

Sweeteners

There are many types of artificial sweetener to choose from, and many have intimidating chemical-sounding names. The sweetener market is a minefield, with positive marketing claims and negative reviews vying for attention.

If you are following a sugar free diet, then my strong recommendation is to experiment with different options, find one that agrees with you taste-wise and digestive-wise, then learn about how best to use it in different applications.

If you are following a low carbohydrate diet, then the situation is not so easy. To try and simplify the ingredient lists in this book, I have used two types of sweeteners: granulated sweetener and sugar free sweetening syrup. Each of these sweeteners has different properties and uses, and although there are many more options available, these are a great starting point.

Granular Sweetener: There is a very wide range to choose from including erythritol blends like Swerve, xylitol, monkfruit blends, stevia, and more.

Deciding on your preferred sweetener is one of the most difficult decisions you'll need to make on a low carb diet, because it's a balance of cost, taste, availability, and any side effects.

Within this book, I have used granular sweeteners that have the same sweetness cup for cup with regular sugar, so you should be able to substitute your own preferred brand with the recipes listed.

Note: Xylitol is harmful to dogs, even in small doses.

Powdered Sweetener: My preferred brand is Swerve confectioner's sweetener, which you can buy from Amazon or Whole Foods.

Sugar Free Sweetening Syrup: Popular brands include Da Vinci and Torani and these are available in a wide range of flavors (although I usually use the chocolate flavor in this book).

These liquid sweeteners (sometimes called "syrups") usually don't contain any carbohydrates: they are sweetened with sucralose.

You can substitute an alternative like liquid stevia, but you will probably only need a fraction of the quantity listed in the recipe.

Chocolate – the different types

There are many kinds of chocolate product available on the market – but most are high in carbohydrates and nearly all contain sugar. Of the sugar free products, there is a huge range in quality – many containing maltitol, which causes digestive issues for many people.

In this book I have used six different ingredients to give the recipes a chocolate flavor. All of them are sugar free! Not every product may be available in stores near you, but they can all be found from online retailers.

Unsweetened Cocoa Powder: Probably the ingredient most frequently used in this book! Easily sourced, either in supermarkets or online. I prefer to use a Dutch-processed variety, because it tends to dissolve into liquids better. Typical Carb Count: 1g net carb per tablespoon

Unsweetened Chocolate: This chocolate is available in solid form (bars or squares) and is 100% cacao. It contains no sugar or dairy products. By itself it can taste very bitter, so sweetener needs to be added to all recipes using unsweetened chocolate. Typical Carb Count: 3g net carbs per 1oz

Chocolate Extract: Made from cocoa beans, water and alcohol, this extract adds depth of flavor to any recipe. If you find any of the recipes in this book not chocolaty enough – try adding some chocolate extract! Typical Carb Count: 0g net carbs per teaspoon

Sugar Free Chocolate Flavor Sweetening Syrup: As mentioned in the sweetener section. Typical Carb Count: 0g net carbs per 2 tablespoons

Sugar Free Baking Chips: Online specialists will usually offer a suitable product. My favorite brand is Lily's Sugar Free Dark Chocolate Mini Baking Chips. They are excellent quality, sweetened with Stevia and are fairly low in carbs. Typical Carb Count: 2g net carbs per 60 chips (½ oz / 14g)

Sugar Free Jello Chocolate Pudding: This pudding mix is fairly low in carbs, and adds both sweetness and chocolate to a recipe in one convenient packet! Typical Carb Count: 6g net carbs per ¼ packet

Key ingredients to get you started

Here are the items used most often in this book – and a great start to getting your kitchen well stocked!

- Unsweetened almond milk (vanilla, plain, or chocolate if you can find it - just make sure it is unsweetened!)
- Unsweetened cocoa powder (as mentioned previously)
- Heavy cream Note: Cashew cream can be a great alternative if you are lactose intolerant
- Eggs
- Almond flour (also called almond meal and ground almonds)
- Sweeteners (see pages 5-6)

Useful kitchen equipment

- Blender or food processor
- Stand mixer
- Ice cream maker
- Large baking sheet
- Measuring cups and spoons

A note about sugar alcohols and nutritional information

Nutritional information for this recipe is provided as a courtesy and is my best approximation. I cannot guarantee completely accurate data due to variations in ingredients and cooking methods.

Carbohydrates from sugar alcohols are not included in net carb counts as it has been shown that they do not impact blood sugar. Net carbs are the total carbs minus fiber.

A note about fat content

If you think of this as a "diet" book, you may be surprised that some of the recipes have a high fat content. However, a moderate amount of fat on a low carbohydrate diet is not only acceptable, but it is often required to keep in ketosis.

Before starting each recipe, I would suggest checking the nutritional data box to confirm if that particular recipe is suitable for your way of eating.

DESSERTS

Chocolate Chia Pudding

Servings: 2

Ingredients

- 1¼ cup unsweetened almond milk
- 2 tbs unsweetened cocoa powder
- 2 tbs sugar free sweetening syrup
- ¼ cup chia seeds

Nutritional Data per serving

Calories 134
Total Fat 8g
Sodium 87mg
Total Carbohydrate 12g
Fiber 10g
Net Carbohydrate 2g
Protein 5g

Directions

1. Add the milk, cocoa and syrup to a blender and mix until the cocoa has been fully incorporated.
2. Pour into a container and add the chia seeds. Mix well, then cover and place in the fridge.
3. Stir after one hour, then return them to the fridge and leave the chia to soak overnight in the chocolate mixture.
4. The next day, stir and serve.

This is a fun breakfast for one person, or a dessert for two to share!

Triple Chocolate Cheese Ball

Servings: 8
Serving Size: ⅛ recipe

Ingredients

- 4 oz unsweetened chocolate
- 2 tbs heavy cream
- 8 oz cream cheese, softened
- ½ cup low carb sweetener
- 1 oz cocoa nibs
- 2 tbs unsweetened cocoa powder

Nutritional Data per serving

Calories 204
Total Fat 20g
Sodium 96mg
Total Carbohydrate 7g
Fiber 3g
Net Carbohydrate 4g
Protein 4g

Directions

1. Melt the unsweetened chocolate and cream together in a bowl, either in the microwave or over a double boiler. Remove from the heat and leave to cool for 10 minutes.
2. Add the chocolate mixture, cream cheese and sweetener to a stand mixer and beat until smooth.
3. Stir in the cocoa nibs, then form the mixture into a ball. Wrap it in plastic wrap and leave in the fridge for at least two hours or overnight.
4. Roll the cheese ball in cocoa powder and serve with toasted low carb tortillas and/or fresh berries.

This sweet cheese ball is great for parties!

Chocolate Brandy Mousse

Servings: 2
Serving Size: ½ recipe

Ingredients

- ½ cup heavy cream
- 1 oz unsweetened chocolate
- ¼ cup cream cheese
- 1-2 tsp brandy
- 1 egg white
- 2 tbs low carb sweetener

Nutritional Data per serving

Calories 386
Total Fat 39g
Sodium 142mg
Total Carbohydrate 7g
Fiber 1g
Net Carbohydrate 6g
Protein 6g

Directions

1. Place the cream and chocolate in a saucepan and melt over a low heat until fully combined.
2. Add the cream cheese, and continue cooking until it has fully melted. Stir in the brandy.
3. In a separate bowl, whisk together the remaining ingredients until stiff peaks form.
4. Carefully fold the egg mixture into the chocolate mixture. Spoon into bowls, cover, and leave in the fridge for at least an hour.

Rum makes a great alternative to brandy in this dessert.

Baked Blueberry Chocolate Pancake

Servings: 2
Serving Size: ½ recipe

Ingredients

- Non-stick cooking spray
- 2 eggs
- ¼ cup almond flour
- 2 tbs heavy cream
- 1 tbs unsweetened cocoa powder
- 1 tbs low carb sweetener
- ¼ tsp baking powder
- ¼ cup fresh blueberries

Nutritional Data per serving

Calories 234
Total Fat 17g
Sodium 139mg
Total Carbohydrate 14g
Fiber 3g
Net Carbohydrate 11g
Protein 10g

Directions

1. Preheat the oven to 375F. Lightly spray a 9" round pie dish with non-stick spray.
2. Add the eggs, almond flour, cream, cocoa, sweetener and baking powder to a medium bowl and whisk to combine.
3. Add the blueberries and pour the mixture into the pie dish. Spread the blueberries out evenly.
4. Bake for 12-15 minutes until the pancake is cooked through. Serve immediately with whipped cream or vanilla yogurt.

This would be a lovely breakfast as well as a dessert!

Mocha Mousse

Servings: 2
Serving Size: ½ recipe

Ingredients

- 1 tbs unsweetened cocoa powder
- 1 tsp freshly ground coffee
- 1 tbs low carb sweetener
- 2 tsp boiling water
- ½ cup heavy cream
- 2 egg whites
- Pinch cream of tartar

Nutritional Data per serving

Calories 229
Total Fat 22g
Sodium 79mg
Total Carbohydrate 5g
Fiber 1g
Net Carbohydrate 4g
Protein 5g

Directions

1. Mix the cocoa, coffee, sweetener and water together in a large bowl. Add the cream and beat with a hand mixer until soft peaks form.
2. In a separate bowl (with clean beaters), whisk the egg whites and cream of tartar together until stiff peaks form.
3. Gently incorporate the egg whites into the cream mixture.
4. Spoon into glasses or bowls and chill in the fridge until required.

You could also try cinnamon instead of coffee!

Cambridge Chocolate Cream

Servings: 2
Serving Size: ½ recipe

Ingredients

- 1 cup heavy cream
- ¼ cup water
- 1 tbs unsweetened cocoa powder
- ½ tsp vanilla extract
- 2 egg yolks
- 2 tbs + 1 tsp low carb sweetener, divided

Nutritional Data per serving

Calories 472
Total Fat 48g
Sodium 53mg
Total Carbohydrate 9g
Fiber 1g
Net Carbohydrate 8g
Protein 5g

Directions

1. Preheat the oven to 300F.
2. Add the cream, cocoa, water and vanilla extract to a saucepan, bring to a boil. Remove from the heat then let cool, stirring occasionally.
3. In a medium bowl, mix together egg yolks and 2 tbs sweetener. In a steady stream, pour in the cooled cream mixture, whisking constantly.
4. Pour the mixture into two ramekins and place in a deep baking tray. Pour water into the tray so that it is half way up the ramekins. Bake for 40-50 minutes until the dessert has set. Let cool.
5. Sprinkle ½ tsp of sweetener onto the surface of each dessert, then place under a broiler. Let the sweetener turn liquid and then caramelize. Remove from the broiler and let cool. Keep in the fridge until required.

This dish is particularly suited to those following a low carb high fat diet.

Rich Chocolate Dessert

Servings: 2
Serving Size: ½ recipe

Ingredients

- ½ cup Ricotta cheese (whole milk)
- ½ cup unsweetened almond milk
- ¼ cup low carb sweetener
- ¼ cup water
- 2 tbs unsweetened cocoa powder
- 1/8 tsp xanthan gum

Nutritional Data per serving

Calories 127
Total Fat 9g
Sodium 89mg
Total Carbohydrate 7g
Fiber 2g
Net Carbohydrate 5g
Protein 8g

Directions

1. Place all the ingredients into a food processor and blend until smooth and thoroughly combined.
2. Spoon the mixture into small bowls, cover, and leave in the fridge until required.

This is such a super quick dessert to prepare!

Chocolate Quesadilla

Servings: 2
Serving Size: ½ recipe

Ingredients

- 2 6" low carb tortillas
- 1 tbs mascarpone cheese
- ½ oz sugar free dark chocolate mini baking chips
- 1 tsp low carb sweetener

Nutritional Data per serving

Calories 115
Total Fat 8g
Sodium 10mg
Total Carbohydrate 12g
Fiber 6g
Net Carbohydrate 6g
Protein 5g

Directions

1. Spread the mascarpone onto one of the tortillas and cover it with the chocolate chips.
2. Cover with the second tortilla and sprinkle the top with half the sweetener.
3. Place in a preheated (dry) frying pan, sweetener side down and cook until the tortilla turns hard. Sprinkle the remaining sweetener over the top and flip the quesadilla over.
4. Cook until the lower tortilla is crispy then serve warm.

This would be the perfect ending to a Mexican meal!

Chocolate Zabaglione

Servings: 2
Serving Size: ½ recipe

Ingredients

- 2 egg yolks
- 2 tbs Marsala (do not substitute with Marsala cooking wine)
- 1 tbs sugar free chocolate flavor sweetening syrup
- 2 tsp low carb sweetener
- 1 tsp unsweetened cocoa powder

Nutritional Data per serving

Calories 77
Total Fat 5g
Sodium 25mg
Total Carbohydrate 5g
Fiber 0.4g
Net Carbohydrate 4.6g
Protein 4g

Directions

1. Make a bain marie by placing a bowl over a small saucepan. Add water to the saucepan and bring it to a simmer, ensuring that the bowl does not touch the water.
2. Add the ingredients to the bowl, and use a small balloon whisk to combine. Whisk continuously until the mixture is thick, foamy, and doubled in volume. This may take 5-10 minutes.
3. Pour the zabaglione into glasses or bowls and serve immediately.

This indulgent dish is worth the effort!

Chocolate Jicama Crunch

Servings: 2
Serving Size: ½ recipe

Ingredients

- 2 tbs unsalted butter
- 2 tbs low carb sweetener
- 1 tsp unsweetened cocoa powder
- ¼ tsp ground cinnamon
- 10 oz peeled and diced jicama

Nutritional Data per serving

Calories 157
Total Fat 11g
Sodium 7mg
Total Carbohydrate 13g
Fiber 7g
Net Carbohydrate 5g
Protein 1g

Directions

1. Add the butter, sweetener, cocoa powder and cinnamon to a saucepan and cook over a low heat until a chocolate sauce has formed.
2. Add the jicama and cook for 15-20 minutes, stirring occasionally. The jicama will remain crunchy, like the texture of a raw apple.
3. Serve warm and see if your guests can guess the mystery ingredient!

The jicama is similar to crunchy apple in this dessert!

LF GF SF LC

Creamy Chocolate Pudding

Servings: 2
Serving Size: ½ recipe

Ingredients

- 1 tsp unflavored unsweetened powdered gelatin
- 1 tbs unsweetened cocoa powder
- ¼ cup boiling water
- ½ cup unsweetened almond milk
- ¼ cup low carb sweetener
- ½ cup cream cheese

Nutritional Data per serving

Calories 206
Total Fat 19g
Sodium 186g
Total Carbohydrate 5g
Fiber 0g
Net Carbohydrate 5g
Protein 5g

Directions

1. In a small bowl, combine the gelatin, cocoa powder and boiling water. Let stand for 5 minutes.
2. Add the cocoa mixture and the remaining ingredients to a food processor or blender and blend until smooth.
3. Pour into two small bowls or glasses. Cover and leave in the fridge to chill for at least an hour.

This pudding would also make a great snack!

Chocolate Crepes

Servings: 2
Serving Size: 3 crepes

Ingredients

- 2 oz cream cheese
- 2 eggs
- 1 tbs low carb sweetener
- 1 tsp unsweetened cocoa powder

Nutritional Data per serving

Calories 185
Total Fat 15g
Sodium 155mg
Total Carbohydrate 8g
Fiber 0g
Net Carbohydrate 8g
Protein 8g

Directions

1. Combine all ingredients in a food processor or blender until smooth.
2. Heat a small frying pan over a medium heat, then spoon in enough of the mixture to just cover the base in a thin layer.
3. Let the crepe cook for about a minute then carefully ease it up at the edges with a spatula and flip it over when it is ready.
4. Transfer the cooked crepe to a plate and repeat with the rest of the mixture. Makes approximately 6 crepes.

These would be amazing for a special brunch!

Light Chocolate Mousse

Servings: 2
Serving Size: ½ recipe

Ingredients

- 1 tsp unflavored unsweetened gelatin powder
- ¼ cup boiling water
- 3 tbs low carb sweetener
- 1 tbs unsweetened cocoa powder
- 2 egg whites
- ¼ tsp cream of tartar

Nutritional Data per serving

Calories 29
Total Fat 0g
Sodium 54mg
Total Carbohydrate 2g
Fiber 0g
Net Carbohydrate 2g
Protein 5g

Directions

1. In a small bowl, mix together the gelatin, water, cocoa and sweetener Whisk until smooth then set aside to cool.
2. In a stand mixer, whisk together the egg whites and cream of tartar until soft peaks form. Add the cooled cocoa mixture and beat at low speed until thoroughly combined.
3. Pour into two bowls, cover, and leave in the fridge to set for at least an hour.

This light and airy mousse can be a wonderful end to a meal.

Avocado Chocolate Pudding

Servings: 2
Serving Size: ½ recipe

Ingredients

- 2 ripe avocados, skin and seed removed
- 4-6 tbs sugar free chocolate flavor sweetening syrup
- ¼ cup water
- 2 tbs unsweetened cocoa powder

Nutritional Data per serving

Calories 301
Total Fat 27g
Sodium 0mg
Total Carbohydrate 18g
Fiber 13g
Net Carbohydrate 5g
Protein 4g

Directions

1. Add all ingredients to a blender or food processor and blend until smooth. Scrape down the sides with a spatula if necessary to ensure even blending.
2. Spoon the mixture into two small bowls.
3. Cover and keep in the fridge until required.

Avocado is so good for you, why not have it for dessert, too?!?

SWEET TREATS

Chocolate Dipped Pecans

Servings: 4
Serving Size: 8 pecan halves

Ingredients

- 42g sugar free dark chocolate mini baking chips
- 32 pecan halves

Nutritional Data per serving

Calories 96
Total Fat 8g
Sodium 0mg
Total Carbohydrate 7g
Fiber 4g
Net Carbohydrate 3g
Protein 1g

Directions

1. Place the chocolate chips in a bowl and microwave in small bursts until melted.
2. Dip each pecan halfway into the melted chocolate, then place on a baking sheet lined with a silicone mat or parchment paper.
3. Let the chocolate set, then transfer to an airtight container and keep cool.

These make great gifts!

Choc-Almond Cheesecake Balls

Servings: 8
Serving Size: One cheesecake ball

Ingredients

- ½ cup cream cheese
- ¼ cup unsweetened natural almond butter
- 2 tbs unsweetened cocoa powder
- 2 tbs sugar free chocolate flavor sweetening syrup
- ¼ cup almond flour

Nutritional Data per serving

Calories 117
Total Fat 11g
Sodium 44mg
Total Carbohydrate 4g
Fiber 2g
Net Carbohydrate 2g
Protein 3g

Directions

1. Mix together the cream cheese, almond butter, cocoa and syrup in a bowl.
2. Chill the mixture for 30 minutes.
3. Form the mixture into 8 balls, then roll them in the almond flour.
4. Keep refrigerated until ready to eat.

Your guests will appreciate these light bites at the end of a meal.

Cocoa Meringue Cookies

Servings: 10
Serving Size: 4 cookies

Ingredients

- 4 egg whites
- ¼ tsp cream of tartar
- ½ cup confectioner's Swerve
- ¼ tsp vanilla extract
- 1 tsp unsweetened cocoa powder

> **Nutritional Data per serving**
>
> Calories 6
> Total Fat 0g
> Sodium 19mg
> Total Carbohydrate 0.2g
> Fiber 0g
> Net Carbohydrate 0.2g
> Protein 1g

Directions

1. Preheat the oven to 200F.
2. Add the egg whites, cream of tartar and sweetener to a stand mixer bowl, then whisk until soft peaks form.
3. Spoon a third of the mixture into a separate bowl and set aside.
4. With the remaining two thirds, add the vanilla and whisk until stiff peaks form. Transfer to a separate bowl.
5. Return the one third mixture to the stand mixer, add the cocoa powder and whisk until stiff peaks form.
6. Fold the vanilla mixture into the cocoa mixture with just a few strokes.
7. Spoon the combined mixture into a piping bag fitted with a large star nozzle. Pipe out onto two baking trays lined with silicone mat or baking parchment. This recipe makes about 40.
8. Bake for one hour, turn off the heat, and leave the meringues in the oven with the door closed for three hours or until crisp.

These meringues keep for weeks!

Yogurt Jello Bites

Servings: 15
Serving Size: 3 bites

Ingredients

- 1 packet sugar free chocolate Jello pudding
- 1½ cups nonfat Greek yogurt
- ½ cup water

Nutritional Data per serving

Calories 22
Total Fat 0g
Sodium 91mg
Total Carbohydrate 3g
Fiber 0g
Net Carbohydrate 3g
Protein 2.6g

Directions

1. Add all ingredients to a saucepan and cook on a low heat, stirring constantly.
2. When all the jello has dissolved, spoon the mixture into small candy molds. This recipe makes about 45 x 1" bites.
3. Place them in the fridge to set. If necessary, transfer them to the freezer for 5 minutes before unmolding.
4. Store in the fridge.

Everyone will enjoy these fat free treats!

LF GF SF LC

Almond Chocolate Truffles

Servings: 18
Serving Size: 1 truffle

Ingredients

- 4 oz unsweetened chocolate
- ½ cup heavy cream
- ¼ cup low carb sweetener
- ¼ cup almond flour
- 2 tbs unsalted butter, melted
- 2 tbs unsweetened cocoa powder

Nutritional Data per serving

Calories 75
Total Fat 7g
Sodium 4mg
Total Carbohydrate 2g
Fiber 1g
Net Carbohydrate 1g
Protein 1g

Directions

1. Melt the chocolate by placing it in a microwave-proof bowl and cooking for 15-30 second bursts, stirring between each burst.
2. Stir the cream, sweetener, almond flour and butter into the chocolate.
3. Place the bowl in the fridge for 30 mins or until firm.
4. Sprinkle the cocoa onto a small plate. Shape the truffle mixture into 18 balls, then roll them in the cocoa powder.
5. Store in an airtight container in the fridge until required.

These truffles taste so indulgent and decadent!

Cocoa Nib Mediants

Servings: 16
Serving Size: 1 mediant

Ingredients

- 3 oz unsweetened chocolate
- ¼ cup unsalted butter
- 2 tbs powdered erythritol (Confectioners Swerve or similar)
- 1 oz raw cocoa nibs

Nutritional Data per serving

Calories 62
Total Fat 6g
Sodium 1mg
Total Carbohydrate 1g
Fiber 1g
Net Carbohydrate 0g
Protein 0g

Directions

1. In a saucepan, melt together the chocolate, butter and sweetener over a low heat. Stir until smooth.
2. Place spoonfuls of the chocolate mixture onto a baking tray lined with a silicone mat or baking parchment. Spread the chocolate around slightly to make 16 small disks. Sprinkle the cocoa nibs over each one.
3. Leave to set.

If you don't have cocoa nibs try toasted nuts instead!

LF GF SF LC

Chocolate Gummy Squares

Servings: 4
Serving Size: 4 squares

Ingredients

- 1½ cups water
- ⅓ cup unsweetened almond milk
- 3 tbs low carb sweetener
- 2 tbs unsweetened cocoa powder
- 2 envelopes (2 tbs) unsweetened powdered gelatin
- 1 tsp chocolate extract

Nutritional Data per serving

Calories 17
Total Fat 0g
Sodium 7mg
Total Carbohydrate 1g
Fiber 0g
Net Carbohydrate 1g
Protein 3g

Directions

1. Add all ingredients to a saucepan, bring to the boil, then simmer. Whisk frequently until the cocoa and gelatin have dissolved.
2. Pour into a non-stick baking tray (8x8") and leave to cool. When cool, transfer to the fridge until set.
3. Cut the jelly into 16 squares and carefully remove from the baking tray.

Kids will love these too!

Coconut Chocolate Bites

Servings: 12
Serving Size: 1 bite

Ingredients

- ½ cup coconut oil
- ½ cup unsweetened almond butter
- 3 tbs unsweetened cocoa powder
- 3 tbs heavy cream
- 2 tbs low carb sweetener

Nutritional Data per serving

Calories 158
Total Fat 16g
Sodium 2mg
Total Carbohydrate 2g
Fiber 1g
Net Carbohydrate 1g
Protein 2g

Directions

1. Add the almond butter and oil to a saucepan over a low heat, and let them melt together.
2. Add the remaining ingredients and stir until smooth.
3. Spoon or pour the mixture into 12 silicone molds. Place in the freezer for 15 minutes, then remove from the mold.
4. Store in the fridge.

These are ideal for anyone following a low carb high fat diet.

Chocolate
Fudge

Servings: 16
Serving Size: 1 square

Ingredients

- ½ cup unsweetened almond milk
- ¾ cup low carb sweetener
- ¼ cup heavy cream
- ¼ cup coconut oil
- 8 oz unsweetened chocolate

Nutritional Data per serving

Calories 114
Total Fat 12g
Sodium 10mg
Total Carbohydrate 4g
Fiber 2g
Net Carbohydrate 2g
Protein 1g

Directions

1. Add the milk, sweetener, cream, and coconut oil to a medium saucepan. Cook over a low heat until fully combined.
2. Break the chocolate into squares and add to the saucepan. Stir frequently until the chocolate has fully dissolved.
3. Pour the mixture into a 8x8" baking dish lined with parchment paper. Let cool then place in the fridge to set.
4. Remove from the fridge and cut into 16 squares.

This fudge is perfect for a sweet snack!

Wasabi Chocolate Truffles

Servings: 12
Serving Size: 1 truffle

Ingredients

- ½ cup heavy cream
- 1 tsp prepared wasabi paste
- 3 tbs powdered erythritol (Confectioners Swerve or similar)
- 3 oz unsweetened chocolate, chopped
- 2 tbs unsweetened cocoa powder

Nutritional Data per serving

Calories 71
Total Fat 7g
Sodium 5mg
Total Carbohydrate 2g
Fiber 1g
Net Carbohydrate 1g
Protein 1g

Directions

1. Add the cream, wasabi and sweetener to a small saucepan. Heat gently and stir until the wasabi has melted into the cream.
2. Turn off the heat and add the chocolate. Stir until it has all dissolved.
3. Pour the mixture into a bowl, leave to cool, then transfer to the fridge for 30 minutes.
4. Form the mixture into 12 balls, roll each one in cocoa powder, and store in the fridge until required.

These truffles have a fiery kick to them!

Cocoa Nuts in the Slow Cooker

Servings: 6
Serving Size: ⅙ recipe

Ingredients

- ½ cup pecan halves
- ½ cup walnut halves
- ½ cup slivered almonds
- 2 tbs unsweetened cocoa powder
- 2 tsp low carb sweetener
- 1 tsp vanilla extract
- 2 tbs unsalted butter, melted

Nutritional Data per serving

Calories 218
Total Fat 21g
Sodium 1mg
Total Carbohydrate 5g
Fiber 3g
Net Carbohydrate 2g
Protein 4g

Directions

1. Place all the ingredients in a small slow cooker and stir well.
2. Cook on high for 1 hour.
3. Spread the cocoa nuts out onto a baking sheet to cool.
4. Store in an airtight container.

These smell fantastic when they are cooking!

BAKED GOODS

Chocolate Peanut Butter Cookies

Servings: 12
Serving Size: 1 cookie

Ingredients

- 1 cup chunky natural peanut butter (unsweetened)
- 2 eggs
- ½ cup unsweetened cocoa powder
- ½ cup low carb sweetener
- 1 tsp baking soda

Nutritional Data per serving

Calories 145
Total Fat 12g
Sodium 214mg
Total Carbohydrate 6g
Fiber 2g
Net Carbohydrate 4g
Protein 7g

Directions

1. Preheat the oven to 350F.
2. Place all ingredients into a food processor and blend until smooth.
3. Using your hands, form the mixture into 12 balls and place them on a baking tray lined with silicone mat or baking parchment. Flatten them into cookie shapes.
4. Bake for 10 minutes. After cooking, leave on the baking tray for at least 10 minutes to cool.

This also works well with smooth peanut butter!

Chocolate Cheesecake Brownies

Servings: 16
Serving Size: 1 brownie

Brownie Ingredients:
- ¼ cup low carb sweetener
- 3 tbs unsalted butter
- ½ cup almond flour
- 1 egg
- 2 tbs unsweetened cocoa powder
- 2 tbs cold water

Cheesecake Ingredients:
- 8oz cream cheese
- 3 tbs low carb sweetener
- 1 egg
- 1 tsp vanilla extract

Nutritional Data per serving

Calories 97
Total Fat 9g
Sodium 53mg
Total Carbohydrate 1g
Fiber 0g
Net Carbohydrate 1g
Protein 2g

Directions

1. Preheat the oven to 350F. Line an 8x8" square baking tin with parchment paper.
2. In a stand mixer, cream together the sweetener and butter. Add the remaining brownie ingredients and beat until thoroughly combined. Spoon the mixture into the prepared tin.
3. In a separate bowl, whisk together the cheesecake ingredients until smooth. Pour the mixture on top of the brownie mixture, and gently swirl them together with a skewer.
4. Bake for 25 minutes or until the topping is firm. Let the brownies cool then turn out onto a cooling rack and cut into 16 squares.

These look so pretty!

Hazelnut Chocolate Pie

Servings: 6
Serving Size: 1 slice

Ingredients

- 1½ cups hazelnut meal
- 4 tbs unsalted butter, melted
- 1 packet Sugar free Jello Chocolate Pudding
- 2 tsp cornstarch
- 1½ cups unsweetened almond milk

Nutritional Data per serving

Calories 295
Total Fat 25g
Sodium 332mg
Total Carbohydrate 11.5g
Fiber 4g
Net Carbohydrate 7.5g
Protein 4g

Directions

1. Mix the hazelnut meal and melted butter together and press into a 9" round pie pan. Place in the fridge for at least one hour.
2. Add the remaining ingredients to a bowl and use a mixer to combine well.
3. Pour into the chilled crust, then cover. Place in the fridge for at least 3 hours or overnight.

Chocolate and hazelnut is such a winning flavor combination.

Mini Chocolate Chip Cupcakes

Servings: 24
Serving Size: 1 cupcake

Ingredients

- 3 eggs
- 1¼ cup almond flour
- 2 tbs low carb sweetener
- ½ tsp baking powder
- 1½ oz sugar free dark chocolate mini baking chips

Nutritional Data per serving

Calories 50
Total Fat 4g
Sodium 19mg
Total Carbohydrate 3g
Fiber 1g
Net Carbohydrate 2g
Protein 2g

Directions

1. Preheat the oven to 350F. Line a 24-hole mini muffin pan with paper cases.
2. Add the eggs, almond flour, baking powder and sweetener to a stand mixer. Beat until smooth.
3. Stir in the chocolate chips, then divide the mixture between the mini muffin cups.
4. Bake for 10-15 minutes until cooked thoroughly.

Everyone loves chocolate chips!

Cinnamon Chocolate Crisps

Servings: 12
Serving Size: 1 crisp

Ingredients

- ¼ cup unsalted butter, room temperature
- ¼ cup cream cheese
- 1 egg
- 2 tbs unsweetened cocoa powder
- 2 tbs low carb sweetener
- ½ tsp ground cinnamon

Nutritional Data per serving

Calories 63
Total Fat 6g
Sodium 21mg
Total Carbohydrate 3g
Fiber 0.5g
Net Carbohydrate 2.5g
Protein 1g

Directions

1. Preheat the oven to 375F. Line a baking sheet with parchment paper or silicone mat.
2. Mix all the ingredients together in a stand mixer until fully combined.
3. Evenly spoon out the mixture into 12 mounds. Bake for 7-10 minutes or until the crisps start to turn dark at the edges.
4. Let cool, then carefully transfer them to a cooling rack. They will become more crispy as they finish cooling.

Try serving these with a dollop of whipped cream!

Chocolate Mug Cake

Servings: 1

Ingredients

- ¼ cup flax meal
- 1 egg
- 1 tbs sugar free chocolate flavor sweetening syrup
- 2 tsp unsweetened cocoa powder
- 1 teaspoon coconut oil
- ½ tsp baking powder

Nutritional Data per serving

Calories 264
Total Fat 19g
Sodium 325mg
Total Carbohydrate 11g
Fiber 9g
Net Carbohydrate 2g
Protein 13g

Directions

1. Add all ingredients to a cup or mug and whisk until smooth.
2. Place in the microwave and cook on high for 1 minute or until the cake is cooked through.
3. Leave for 1 minute, then enjoy!

The perfect quick pick-me-up!

Chocolate Amaretti

Servings: 12
Serving Size: 1 amaretti

Ingredients

- 1 egg white
- ¼ cup low carb sweetener
- 2 tsp unsweetened cocoa powder
- pinch cream of tartar
- ½ cup almond flour
- 1 tsp almond extract
- 12 pieces of sliced almond

Nutritional Data per serving

Calories 40
Total Fat 2g
Sodium 4mg
Total Carbohydrate 5g
Fiber 1g
Net Carbohydrate 4g
Protein 1g

Directions

1. Preheat the oven to 325F. Line a baking sheet with parchment paper or a silicone mat.
2. In a medium bowl, whisk the egg white, sweetener, cocoa and cream of tartar until stiff peaks form.
3. Stir in the almond flour and almond extract.
4. Drop 12 spoonfuls of the mixture onto the baking sheet, evenly spaced. Place a sliced almond on each mound.
5. Bake for 15 minutes or until starting to turn darker brown at the edges. Leave to cool for 10 minutes then transfer to a cooling rack. Leave on the rack until crisp, then store in an airtight container.

LC SF GF LF

Serve these with a cup of coffee for an afternoon treat!

Individual Chocolate Cheesecakes

Servings: 6
Serving Size: 1 cheesecake

Ingredients

- 8 oz cream cheese
- 1 egg
- 3 tbs low carb sweetener
- 2 tbs unsweetened cocoa powder

Nutritional Data per serving

Calories 143
Total Fat 13g
Sodium 132mg
Total Carbohydrate 2g
Fiber 0g
Net Carbohydrate 2g
Protein 3g

Directions

1. Preheat the oven to 350F.
2. Add all ingredients to a stand mixer and blend until smooth.
3. Spoon into a 6-hole lined muffin pan and bake for 15 minutes or until cooked through.
4. Let cool, then store in the fridge.

Add a flavored extract for variety!

Raspberry Chocolate Mini Muffins

Servings: 24
Serving Size: 1 mini muffin

Ingredients

- 2 cups almond flour
- 2 eggs
- 2 egg whites
- ¼ cup low carb sweetener
- 2 tbs unsweetened cocoa powder
- 2 tbs coconut oil
- 1 tsp baking powder
- 1 cup fresh raspberries

Nutritional Data per serving

Calories 72
Total Fat 6g
Sodium 9mg
Total Carbohydrate 3g
Fiber 1g
Net Carbohydrate 2g
Protein 2g

Directions

1. Preheat the oven to 350F.
2. Mix all ingredients apart from the raspberries in a food processor until smooth.
3. Chop the raspberries roughly into quarters, then stir into the muffin mixture.
4. Spoon the mixture equally between a 24-hole mini muffin pan lined with paper cases.
5. Bake for 15-20 minutes until cooked through. Transfer to a wire cooling rack.

You could also try blackberries or blueberries!

Pecan Chocolate Brownies

Servings: 8
Serving Size: 2 squares

Ingredients

- ½ cup unsalted butter, softened
- ¼ cup low carb sweetener
- 2 eggs
- ¼ cup unsweetened cocoa powder
- ¾ cup finely chopped pecans

Nutritional Data per serving

Calories 194
Total Fat 20g
Sodium 117g
Total Carbohydrate 3g
Fiber 1g
Net Carbohydrate 2g
Protein 2g

Directions

1. Preheat the oven to 350F. Line an 8x8" square baking tin with a silicone mat or baking parchment.
2. Add the butter and sweetener to a stand mixer and beat until smooth.
3. Add the eggs and cocoa, beat again until everything has been incorporated.
4. Stir in the pecans, then pour into the prepared baking tin. Bake for 20 minutes until firm at the edges and slightly soft in the center.
5. Leave to cool for 10 minutes then transfer to a cooling rack. Cut into 16 squares.

These brownies are so soft and squidgy!

LF GF SF LC

Coconut Chocolate Cookies

Servings: 12
Serving Size: 1 cookie

Ingredients

- ¼ cup coconut flour
- 2 tbs unsweetened cocoa powder
- ½ tsp baking powder
- 3 tbs coconut oil
- 2 tbs unsalted butter, softened
- 2 eggs, beaten
- ¼ cup low carb sweetener

Nutritional Data per serving

Calories 69
Total Fat 6g
Sodium 32mg
Total Carbohydrate 2g
Fiber 1g
Net Carbohydrate 1g
Protein 1g

Directions

1. Preheat the oven to 375F.
2. Sift the coconut flour, cocoa powder and baking powder into a bowl and set aside.
3. In a separate bowl, beat the oil and butter together until smooth. Add the eggs and sweetener and stir well.
4. Add the dry ingredients to the wet, and mix well to combine.
5. Spoon the mixture onto a baking tray lined with a silicone mat or parchment paper, and bake for 8-10 minutes or until the edges start to turn darker brown.

Store these cookies in an airtight container.

Basic Chocolate Cake

Servings: 6
Serving Size: 1 slice

Ingredients

- 2 eggs, separated
- ¼ cup heavy cream
- 2 tbs unsalted butter, melted
- 2 tbs unsweetened cocoa powder
- 2 tbs low carb sweetener
- 1 tsp baking powder
- ½ cup almond flour

Nutritional Data per serving

Calories 146
Total Fat 13g
Sodium 59mg
Total Carbohydrate 3g
Fiber 1g
Net Carbohydrate 2g
Protein 4g

Directions

1. Preheat the oven to 350F. Line and grease a 9" round cake tin.
2. In a large bowl, mix together the yolks, cream, melted butter, cocoa, sweetener and baking powder until smooth. Stir in the almond flour.
3. In a separate bowl, use a stand mixer or electric mixer to whisk the egg whites until soft peaks form.
4. Add a large spoonful of the egg whites into the cocoa mixture to loosen it up, then fold in the remaining egg whites.
5. Pour the mixture into the cake tin and bake for 13-15 minutes until cooked through. Cool for 5 minutes then transfer to a cooling rack.

Finish this cake with whipped cream or chocolate frosting!

FROZEN TREATS

Chocolate Pudding Pops

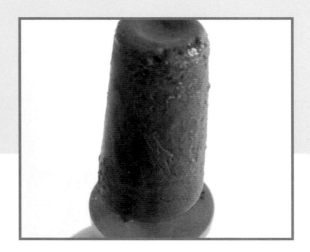

Servings: 7
Serving Size: 1 pop

Ingredients

- 1 packet Sugar Free Chocolate Jello Pudding
- 2 cups unsweetened almond milk

Nutritional Data per serving

Calories 28
Total Fat 0.7g
Sodium 222mg
Total Carbohydrate 5g
Fiber 1g
Net Carbohydrate 4g
Protein 1g

Directions

1. Add both ingredients to a bowl and whisk for two minutes.

2. Pour into popsicle molds and freeze until the pops are solid.

3. Hold the mold under running warm water to help release the pop.

Kids will love these pops too!

Mint Chocolate Ice Cream

Servings: 4
Serving Size: ¼ recipe

Ingredients

- 1 cup heavy cream
- ¼ cup unsweetened cocoa powder
- ½ cup low carb sweetener
- 2 tbs ricotta
- ¼ tsp peppermint extract
- 1 tsp chocolate extract, optional

Nutritional Data per serving

Calories 230
Total Fat 23g
Sodium 30mg
Total Carbohydrate 6g
Fiber 1g
Net Carbohydrate 5g
Protein 3g

Directions

1. In a stand mixer, combine the cream and cocoa until frothy.
2. Add all the remaining ingredients and continue to mix until well combined and very thick.
3. Transfer the mixture to an ice cream machine and churn according to manufacturer's instructions.

Mint and chocolate is such a refreshing combination!

Tequila Chocolate Granita

Servings: 4
Serving Size: ¼ recipe

Ingredients

- 2 cups water
- ¼ cup low carb sweetener
- ¼ cup unsweetened cocoa powder
- 2 tbs tequila

Nutritional Data per serving

Calories 29
Total Fat 0g
Sodium 1mg
Total Carbohydrate 3g
Fiber 1g
Net Carbohydrate 2g
Protein 1g

Directions

1. Add all the ingredients to a saucepan, stir and cook over a medium heat until the cocoa powder has dissolved.
2. Pour into a shallow container and let cool.
3. Place in the freezer, stirring the mixture after two hours. Stir again after another hour to distribute the ice crystals.
4. After another hour, rake the mixture with a fork to form loose chunks.

The texture of a granita is coarser than regular ice cream.

Chocolate Chip Ice Cream

Servings: 6
Serving Size: ⅙ recipe

Ingredients

- 2 cups heavy cream
- 1 cup unsweetened almond milk
- ½ cup low carb sweetener
- 2 tsp vanilla extract
- 1½ oz sugar free dark chocolate mini baking chips

Nutritional Data per serving

Calories 277
Total Fat 29g
Sodium 30mg
Total Carbohydrate 2g
Fiber 0g
Net Carbohydrate 2g
Protein 1g

Directions

1. Add the cream, milk, sweetener and extract to a bowl and stir well to mix.
2. Pour into an ice cream maker and let it run until crystals start to form.
3. Stir in the baking chips, pour into a container and freeze until the ice cream has reached soft scoop stage.

The chocolate chips add a fun pop to this delicious ice cream!

Frozen Orange Chocolate Creams

Servings: 12
Serving Size: 2 creams

Ingredients

- 1 cup heavy cream
- ¼ cup unsweetened cocoa powder
- 2 tbs low carb sweetener
- ½ tsp orange extract

Nutritional Data per serving

Calories 72
Total Fat 7g
Sodium 7mg
Total Carbohydrate 1g
Fiber 0g
Net Carbohydrate 1g
Protein 0g

Directions

1. Add all ingredients to a stand mixer bowl and stir to combine.
2. Whisk until stiff peaks have formed.
3. Spoon the mixture into a piping bag and pipe out swirls onto a baking sheet lined with a silicone mat or baking parchment. This recipe will make approximately 24 swirls with 1" diameter.
4. Place in the freezer for one hour.

These can be eaten straight out of the freezer!

Chocolate Ice Cream

Servings: 6
Serving Size: ⅙ recipe

Ingredients

- 1 envelope (1 tbs) unsweetened powdered gelatin
- ¼ cup water
- 1½ cups heavy cream
- 1 cup unsweetened almond milk
- 6 tbs unsweetened cocoa powder
- ½ cup low carb sweetener

Nutritional Data per serving

Calories 226
Total Fat 23g
Sodium 46mg
Total Carbohydrate 5g
Fiber 1g
Net Carbohydrate 4g
Protein 3g

Directions

1. In a small bowl, mix together the gelatin and water.
2. Add the remaining ingredients to a saucepan and place over a low heat.
3. Add the gelatin mixture and whisk until everything has dissolved.
4. Simmer for five minutes then let cool to room temperature, stirring occasionally.
5. Transfer to an ice cream maker and follow the manufacturer's instructions.

The gelatin in this recipe helps keep the ice cream soft.

Chocolate Chip Balls

Servings: 16
Serving Size: 1 ball

Ingredients

- ¼ cup unsweetened cocoa powder
- ¼ cup water
- 8 oz cream cheese, room temperature
- 4 oz unsalted butter, room temp
- ½ cup low carb sweetener
- ¼ cup sugar free dark chocolate mini baking chips

Nutritional Data per serving

Calories 80
Total Fat 6g
Sodium 100mg
Total Carbohydrate 3.4g
Fiber 1g
Net Carbohydrate 2.4g
Protein 2g

Directions

1. Mix together the cocoa powder and water in the bowl of a stand mixer until a thick paste has formed.
2. Add the cream cheese, butter and sweetener, and blend until smooth.
3. Stir in the chocolate chips.
4. Form the mixture into 16 balls approx 1" diameter. Place on tray or pan lined with a silicone mat or baking parchment.
5. Freeze for one hour before transferring to a lidded container.
6. Remove from the freezer 10 minutes before eating.

These ice cream balls are such fun!

DRINKS

Breakfast Shake

Servings: 1

Ingredients

- ¼ cup plain Greek yogurt
- 1 cup unsweetened almond milk
- 1 tbs flaxseed meal
- 2 tbs unsweetened cocoa powder
- 1 tbs sugar free chocolate flavor sweetening syrup

Nutritional Data per serving

Calories 139
Total Fat 8g
Sodium 153mg
Total Carbohydrate 12g
Fiber 6g
Net Carbohydrate 6g
Protein 10g

Directions

1. Mix all ingredients in a blender until smooth.
2. Taste and adjust sweetness as necessary.

Start the day with this filling chocolate shake!

Mexican Hot Chocolate

Servings: 1

Ingredients

- ½ oz unsweetened chocolate
- 1 cup unsweetened almond milk
- 2 tbs low carb sweetener
- ½ tsp ground cinnamon
- cayenne, to taste

Nutritional Data per serving

Calories 104
Total Fat 9g
Sodium 128mg
Total Carbohydrate 6g
Fiber 3g
Net Carbohydrate 3g
Protein 2g

Directions

1. Add all ingredients to a saucepan and heat over a low heat until the chocolate has melted.
2. Whisk until smooth, then serve immediately.

This will really warm you up on a cold day!

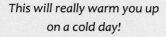

Almond Hot Chocolate

Servings: 1

Ingredients

- ¾ cup unsweetened almond milk
- 2 tsp unsweetened cocoa powder
- 1-2 tbs sugar free chocolate flavor sweetening syrup

Nutritional Data per serving

Calories 30
Total Fat 2g
Sodium 131mg
Total Carbohydrate 3g
Fiber 2g
Net Carbohydrate 1g
Protein 1g

Directions

1. Mix all ingredients together in a saucepan and stir until the cocoa has fully dissolved. Check for sweetness and add more syrup if desired.
2. Heat over a medium heat until preferred temperature is reached, then pour into a cup and enjoy!

This recipe is SUPER low in carbohydrates!

Peanut Butter and Chocolate Shake

Servings: 1

Ingredients

- 1 cup unsweetened almond milk
- 1 tbs creamy unsweetened peanut butter
- 1 tbs unsweetened cocoa powder
- 2 tbs sugar free chocolate flavor sweetening syrup
- Crushed ice, to serve

Nutritional Data per serving

Calories 142
Total Fat 11g
Sodium 223mg
Total Carbohydrate 7g
Fiber 4g
Net Carbohydrate 3g
Protein 5g

Directions

1. Place all the ingredients except the ice in a blender and blend until smooth.
2. Add the ice to a glass and pour in the milkshake.

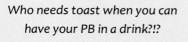

Who needs toast when you can have your PB in a drink?!?

Chocolate Cream Soda

Servings: 1

Ingredients

- ½ cup unsweetened almond milk
- 2-3 tbs sugar free chocolate flavor sweetening syrup
- ½ cup soda water or seltzer water
- Ice

Nutritional Data per serving

Calories 15
Total Fat 1.3g
Sodium 95mg
Total Carbohydrate 0.4g
Fiber 0.4g
Net Carbohydrate 0g
Protein 0.5g

Directions

1. In a tall glass, add the milk and syrup and stir well to mix.

2. Add the water and mix again. Check for sweetness and add more syrup if desired.

3. Serve with ice cubes.

This zero carb drink is perfect for a summer's day.

Chocolate Peppermint Cocktail

Servings: 1

Ingredients

- 2 tbs vodka
- 3 tbs sugar free chocolate flavor sweetening syrup
- 1 tbs heavy cream
- ¼ tsp peppermint extract
- ice

Optional
- low carb sweetener
- red food dye

Nutritional Data per serving

Calories 115
Total Fat 5g
Sodium 25mg
Total Carbohydrate 5g
Fiber 0g
Net Carbohydrate 5g
Protein 0g

Directions

1. To decorate the glass, mix the sweetener and red dye together on a plate. Add a little sugar free syrup to a paper towel then wipe it around the rim of a cocktail glass. Dip the glass into the dyed sweetener.
2. In a cocktail shaker, mix together the remaining ingredients.
3. Add some ice cubes to the prepared glass and pour the shaken cocktail over the top of the ice.

The perfect way to celebrate over the holidays!

Coconut Hot Chocolate

Servings: 1

Ingredients

- ⅓ cup unsweetened coconut milk
- ⅓ cup water
- 2 tbs sugar free chocolate flavor sweetening syrup
- 1 tb unsweetened cocoa powder
- ¼ tsp ground cinnamon
- Unsweetened coconut flakes and cinnamon stick to garnish

Nutritional Data per serving

Calories 149
Total Fat 13g
Sodium 37mg
Total Carbohydrate 6g
Fiber 2g
Net Carbohydrate 4g
Protein 2g

Directions

1. Combine all ingredients on a small saucepan. Whisk or stir over a low heat until the cocoa has dissolved and desired temperature is reached.
2. Serve immediately, garnished with the coconut and cinnamon stick, if desired.

LC SF GF LF

Try this hot chocolate if you're feeling in a tropical mood!

Chocolate Milk Powder

Servings: 24
Serving Size: 2 tsp

Ingredients

- ½ cup low carb sweetener
- ¼ cup unsweetened cocoa powder

Nutritional Data per serving

Calories 11.1
Total Fat 0g
Sodium 0.2mg
Total Carbohydrate 1g
Fiber 0g
Net Carbohydrate 1g
Protein 0g

Directions

1. Add the sweetener and cocoa powder to a screw top jar and shake until fully mixed.
2. Mix 2 teaspoons of the powder with your choice of milk (not included in nutritional data), either by shaking it in a bottle with a lid, or by using an immersion blender.

This powder can also be used to make hot cocoa!

LF GF SF LC

Chocolate Ice Cream Cocktail

Servings: 1

Ingredients

- 1 serving (approx. ½ cup) Chocolate Ice Cream (page 59)
- 2 tbs sugar free chocolate flavor sweetening syrup
- 1 tbs vodka
- Ice

Nutritional Data per serving

Calories 299
Total Fat 23g
Sodium 60mg
Total Carbohydrate 10g
Fiber 2g
Net Carbohydrate 8g
Protein 4g

Directions

1. Add the ice cream, syrup and vodka to a blender and pulse until fully combined.
2. Add some ice to a glass and pour the cocktail over the ice. Serve immediately.

A drink and dessert at the same time!

SAUCES

Chocolate Whipped Cream

Servings: 2
Serving Size: ½ recipe

Ingredients

- ½ cup heavy cream
- 2 tbs unsweetened cocoa powder
- 2 tbs sugar free chocolate flavor sweetening syrup

Nutritional Data per serving

Calories 217
Total Fat 23g
Sodium 29mg
Total Carbohydrate 4g
Fiber 2g
Net Carbohydrate 2g
Protein 2g

Directions

1. Add all ingredients to the bowl of a stand mixer and whisk slowly to incorporate the cocoa.
2. Turn up the speed and whisk until stiff peaks have formed.
3. Spoon the cream into a bowl. Serve immediately or store (covered) in the fridge for up to four hours.

Serve this cream with fresh fruit for a wonderful summer dessert.

Hot Fudge Sauce

Servings: 4
Serving Size: ¼ recipe

Ingredients

- 2 tbs unsalted butter
- ½ cup unsweetened almond milk
- ¼ cup heavy cream
- ¼ cup low carb sweetener
- 3 tbs unsweetened cocoa powder
- ¼ tsp xanthan gum

Nutritional Data per serving

Calories 115
Total Fat 12g
Sodium 28mg
Total Carbohydrate 3g
Fiber 1g
Net Carbohydrate 2g
Protein 1g

Directions

1. Place the butter, milk and cream into a saucepan and heat gently until the butter has melted.
2. Add the remaining ingredients and stir until the cocoa powder has fully dissolved and the sauce has thickened.

This warm sauce feels so indulgent!

Chocolate Barbecue Sauce

Servings: 4
Serving Size: ¼ recipe

Ingredients

- 8 oz canned tomato sauce
- 2 tbs vinegar
- 2 tbs sugar free chocolate flavor sweetening syrup
- 2 tsp dry mustard
- 1 tsp paprika
- 1 tsp chocolate extract
- 1 tsp liquid smoke

Nutritional Data per serving

Calories 22
Total Fat 0g
Sodium 440mg
Total Carbohydrate 5g
Fiber 1.2g
Net Carbohydrate 3.8g
Protein 0g

Directions

1. Add all the ingredients to a saucepan and mix well. Bring to the boil then reduce to a simmer for 5 minutes.
2. Serve immediately or for best results cover and refrigerate the sauce overnight to allow the flavors to develop.

Try this sauce over ribs!

Chocolate Butter

Servings: 6
Serving Size: ⅙ recipe

Ingredients

- 4 oz unsalted butter
- 2 tbs unsweetened cocoa powder
- 1 tbs powdered erythritol (Confectioners Swerve or similar)
- 1 tsp vanilla or chocolate extract

Nutritional Data per serving

Calories 141
Total Fat 15g
Sodium 2mg
Total Carbohydrate 1g
Fiber 0g
Net Carbohydrate 1g
Protein 0g

Directions

1. Add all ingredients to a stand mixer and blend slowly to start mixing everything together.
2. Increase the speed and beat until the butter is smooth.
3. Transfer to a small bowl and store in the fridge (covered) until required.

Spread this amazing butter on just about anything!!

Milk Chocolate Sauce

Servings: 2
Serving Size: ½ recipe

Ingredients

- ½ cup unsweetened almond milk
- 2 tbs heavy cream
- 2 tbs unsweetened cocoa powder
- 2 tbs sugar free chocolate flavor sweetening syrup
- 1 tsp chocolate extract
- Pinch xanthan gum

Nutritional Data per serving

Calories 71
Total Fat 7g
Sodium 54mg
Total Carbohydrate 4g
Fiber 2g
Net Carbohydrate 2g
Protein 2g

Directions

1. Add the milk, cream, cocoa, syrup and extract to a blender and blend until smooth.
2. Sprinkle over the xanthan gum and blend again.
3. Transfer to a small sauce pan and cook over a low heat until the sauce starts to thicken.
4. Serve immediately or let cool then cover and store in the fridge.

*The xanthan gum makes
the sauce thicker.*

Mascarpone Chocolate Sauce

Servings: 6
Serving Size: ⅙ recipe

Ingredients

- ½ cup mascarpone cheese
- 3-4 tbs sugar free chocolate flavor sweetening syrup
- 1 tsp chocolate extract

Nutritional Data per serving

Calories 80
Total Fat 8g
Sodium 10mg
Total Carbohydrate 0g
Fiber 0g
Net Carbohydrate 0g
Protein 0g

Directions

1. Add the ingredients to a bowl and whisk until smooth. Taste for sweetness and add more syrup if required.
2. This sauce can be used instead of ice cream or whipped cream with any fruit dessert, or would make an excellent filling for a layered cake.

Try serving this zero carb sauce with fresh strawberries!

Chocolate Balsamic Vinaigrette

Servings: 4
Serving Size: ½ recipe

Ingredients

- 1 tbs balsamic vinegar
- 1 tbs sugar free chocolate flavor sweetening syrup
- ½ tsp chocolate extract
- ¼ tsp Dijon mustard
- 2 tbs olive oil
- black pepper, optional

Nutritional Data per serving

Calories 62
Total Fat 7g
Sodium 10mg
Total Carbohydrate 0.5g
Fiber 0g
Net Carbohydrate 0.5g
Protein 0g

Directions

1. In a small bowl, whisk together everything except the oil.
2. Slowly drizzle the olive oil into the bowl, whisking constantly and vigorously so that the dressing emulsifies.
3. Check the seasoning and add black pepper if desired.

Try this vinaigrette with a delicious spinach salad!

Creamy Chocolate Frosting

Servings: 12
Serving Size: 1/12 of whole recipe

Ingredients

- ¼ cup heavy cream
- ¼ cup low carb sweetener
- 2 tbs unsweetened cocoa powder

Nutritional Data per serving

Calories 19
Total Fat 1g
Sodium 2mg
Total Carbohydrate 0.2g
Fiber 0g
Net Carbohydrate 0.2g
Protein 0g

Directions

1. Place all ingredients into a stand mixer and beat until stiff peaks form.
2. Spread the mixture onto cupcakes or muffins, then leave at room temperature to set.
3. This recipe covers 12 mini muffins, 6 regular muffins/cupcakes or 1 cake.

Try this frosting over the mini choc chip cupcakes on p43!

Chocolate Custard Sauce

Servings: 2
Serving Size: ½ recipe

Ingredients

- 1 egg yolk
- 3 tbs low carb sweetener
- ½ cup unsweetened almond milk
- ½ oz unsweetened chocolate

Nutritional Data per serving

Calories 71
Total Fat 6g
Sodium 37mg
Total Carbohydrate 3g
Fiber 1g
Net Carbohydrate 2g
Protein 2g

Directions

1. Mix the egg yolk and sweetener together in a small bowl and set aside.
2. Add the milk and chocolate to a bowl and place it over a saucepan of simmering water. Melt the chocolate into the milk, stirring frequently.
3. Add a spoonful of the chocolate mixture to the egg mixture, stir well, then pour it back into the chocolate mixture.
4. Cook for a further 10 minutes, stirring frequently, until the sauce has thickened.
5. Serve immediately.

The egg yolk gives this sauce a really rich flavor.

Coconut Chocolate Sauce

Servings: 4
Serving Size: ¼ recipe

Ingredients

- 2 tbs coconut oil
- 4 tbs unsweetened cocoa powder
- 1 tsp chocolate extract
- 2 tbs water
- 1 tbs sugar free chocolate flavor sweetening syrup

Nutritional Data per serving

Calories 77
Total Fat 7g
Sodium 2mg
Total Carbohydrate 3g
Fiber 2g
Net Carbohydrate 1g
Protein 1g

Directions

1. Place the coconut oil in a bowl and melt it in the microwave.
2. Add the remaining ingredients and whisk until smooth.

This sauce will start to set when poured over ice cream!

RESOURCES

US Online Suppliers*

LC Foods www.lowcarbfoods.com
Fresh baked products, savory essentials, baking essentials, sweet essentials and lots more!

Netrition www. netrition.com
Tons of low carb and sugar free products here including baking mixes, sweeteners, snacks, candy and more.

Amazon.com
Amazon offers a surprisingly large amount of sugar free and low carb products – often with free shipping. Prices are often better when buying in bulk.

Nuts.com
As well as featuring every kind of nut you can imagine, they also stock loads of herbs, spices, and dried fruit. Everything comes in generic packaging but quality and price is great!

Canadian Online Suppliers*

Low Carb Grocery www.thelowcarbgrocery.com
A huge range of low carb products!

Low Carb Canada www.lowcarbcanada.ca
Full range of snack bars, bakery items, condiments, pasta alternatives and more. Plus they have bulk buy offers too!

Amazon.ca
Amazon offers a surprisingly large amount of sugar free and low carb products – often with free shipping. Prices are often better when buying in bulk.

UK Companies*

Sugar Free Megastore www.sugarfreemegastore.com
So many sugar free products to choose from!

Amazon.co.uk
Amazon offers a surprisingly large amount of sugar free and low carb products – often with free shipping. Prices are often better when buying in bulk.

*details correct at time of going to press

Oven Temperature Conversion

°F	°C	Gas
225	110	¼
250	130	½
275	140	1
300	150	2
325	165	3
350	177	4
375	190	5
400	200	6

Egg Yolks and Egg Whites
Got spare yolks or whites? Here's a guide to show you where they can be used:

Recipes that use egg yolks:
Pages 17, 20, 80

Recipes that use egg whites:
Pages 14, 16, 24, 30, 46, 48

INDEX

Triple Chocolate Cheese Ball, p13

ABOUT THE AUTHOR

Georgina is owner and writer for the blog StepAwayFromTheCarbs.com which she started in 2014. It features low carb recipes, information and product reviews. She is also the author of *Low Carb Family Favorites*, *Low Carb Meals For One*, and *Low Carb Snacks.*

She started following a low carb diet in 2008 and enjoys sharing the recipes she creates with others.

Originally from the UK, she now lives in the US with her husband, son and two dogs.

www.stepawayfromthecarbs.com

www.facebook.com/stepawayfromthecarbs/

www.twitter.com/stepawaycarbs

www.pinterest.com/stepawaycarbs/

www.instagram.com/stepawayfromthecarbs/

Made in the USA
Monee, IL
24 May 2021